CHILD OF THE OCMULGEE

The Selected Poems of
Freda Quenneville

Child of the

Edited by

GARRICK DAVIS

Michigan State University Press
East Lansing

Copyright © 2002 by Garrick Davis

⊗ The paper used in this publication meets the minimum
requirements of ANSI/NISO z39.48–1992 (R 1997)
(Permanence of Paper).

Michigan State University Press
East Lansing, Michigan 48823–5202

Printed and bound in the United States of America.

07 06 05 04 03 02 01   1 2 3 4 5 6 7 8 9 10

LIBRARY OF CONGRESS CATALOGING-IN-PUBLICATION DATA

Quenneville, Freda, 1937–1996.

Child of the Ocmulgee: the selected poems of Freda
Quenneville: poems / by Freda Quenneville; edited by
Garrick Davis.

p. cm.

ISBN 0-87013-610-0 (pbk. : alk. paper)

1. Washington (State) — Poetry. 2. Georgia — Poetry.
3. Nature — Poetry. I. Davis, Garrick. II. Title.

PS3567.U2828 C48 2002

811'.54 — DC21

2002006985

Cover photograph of Snoqualmie Falls ©Mary Randlett
    and is used courtesy of the photographer
Cover design by Ariana Grabec-Dingman
Book design by Valerie Brewster, Scribe Typography

Visit Michigan State University Press
on the World Wide Web at:
www.msupress.msu.edu

Contents

PART I

Georgia Childhood

Final Ascent

ACKNOWLEDGMENTS

Grateful acknowledgment is made to the editors of the following journals in which these poems, sometimes in earlier versions, first appeared:

Assay: "The Split in the River" and "The Shot Across Water"

Black Warrior Review: "Having Begonias"

Choice: "The Fireflies"

Confluence: "Hurricane at Bayou Teche" and "A Catch of Crawfish"

Pacific Review: "Washington Pass, North Cascades Highway," "Dharamsala" and "Rituals On the Malabar Coast, India"

Poetry Northwest: "Song," "One Heart, Last Seen," and "Magnolia"

Puget Soundings: "A Pig Tale"

The Quince: "Ocmulgee Winters"

The Raven Chronicles: "Snoqualmie Falls"

The author wished especially to thank her daughters Teresa Quenneville, Suzette Lizotte, and Michelle Hall for their love and inspiration; and Louis Bode, Henry Carlile, Barbara Davidson, Andrew Grob, Randy Morris, Duane Niatum, Mary Randlett, and Robert Sund for their encouragement; she remembered with gratitude her former teachers Grant Redford, Elizabeth Bishop, and Nelson Bentley.

The editor wishes especially to thank Mary Randlett for her devotion to the author and her work, and for the photographs she generously provided. He would also express his gratitude to the author. A few days before her death, she directed her daughters to send her life's work to a virtual stranger, with whom she had exchanged a few letters. That was an act of friendship and of faith, and the editor has tried to be worthy of it. In return, he would present this book to her as a gift, in the hope that he had served her and served her well.

CHILD OF THE OCMULGEE

Introduction

Sometime in September of 1994 (unless it was October or November), a bundle of poems arrived in the mailbox of the *Pacific Review,* a literary journal for which I was serving as editor—but I was a little Nero really. Full of hubris, and programmatic demands concerning poetry, I had dashed off a letter to our contributors asking, nay *demanding,* that they not send us *nature* poetry. For *nature* poetry was everything execrable and stereotyped in the art: the last outpost of High Romantic apostrophizing onanism, that standard pose of tenured hippies in every English department, who peddled their mystical unions with wild daisies (or sycamore trees, or bluebirds, or bluebirds on sycamore trees) to every small magazine in the country. The genre had become a cottage industry: both a long-standing compliment to, and an indictment of, Wordsworth's influence. And so it was, in the fall of that year, that one editor felt the confidence of the blessèd in proclaiming his bull.

Ms. Quenneville did not, of course, receive the letter. Among the poems I read that fall day was "Washington Pass, North Cascades Highway" and its effect on me was evident even several days later, when I wrote to her, accepting it for publication:

> Well, have you stuck me in one hell of a predicament! I've been trumpeting the death of nature poetry for a while and refusing to publish it, and asking that it not be sent to our journal, when I read your poems. "Washington Pass" is the best nature stuff I've read since Frost's "The Most of It."

What had prompted such enthusiasm? A voice, veering between detailed narrative and abstract statement seamlessly, sure-footed even among the irregular line-lengths and slant rhymes:

> I wade alone up a nearby stream,
> a tree-lined cradle of minnows

in the sand of the flood plain.
God is not a question nor absence.

Being a gluttonous man by nature, I immediately asked for more poems. Ms. Quenneville wrote back promptly, enthusiastic about my enthusiasm. I accepted another from this second packet and asked again for more, and each time there was at least one piece of verse that could not be ignored, like "Dharamsala." A random stanza should prove the point:

The Dhaula Dhar, in eternal snow,
stands halfway up the sky.
Blossoming cherries cast
a net across the depths;
pines and ban oaks lean
like madronas on the bluffs at home.

The reader can judge whether I was seized by hyperbole in a weak moment. Certainly, by the third packet or so, I felt in my vanity that I had discovered someone whose connection to nature was not literary, whose imagery was usually faultless, whose tone was often sure. The irony of the whole situation was not lost on me. But, of course, I did not discover her; I was only the latest of her admirers.

Freda Quenneville was a secretary in the King County Department of Public Works, a divorced mother of four, and a well published poet when I met her. She had done readings at universities, won awards, written articles for magazines, written lyrics for choirs. She had studied under Elizabeth Bishop, and been published in the right reviews. In short, there was a career as a regional poet, as a minor bard of the Northwest, pursued quietly and haltingly through three decades, between the demands of a family and a job. Each year a few poems appeared, it seems, wherever the post took them. In 1970, she came "within two hairs' breadths" of having a manuscript accepted at Louisiana State University Press. Twenty-six years later, she had come no closer.

Why this should be an unlikely fate for Freda Quenneville is a story worth recounting. In 1960, as a young wife recently transplanted from Indiana, she had enrolled in night classes at the University of Washington and quickly gravitated to the poetry workshop run by Nelson Bentley. There, her talent was obvious from the first. And though she numbered Rilke, Yeats, and Plath among her favorite poets, her master was Theodore Roethke:

> Over toward Parrington Hall,
> a grove of madrona and elm
> are letting their leaves fall.
>
> The grass is dense green,
> and in light washed clear by rain,
> the trees are swirls that lean
>
> apart from the crowded walkways.
> It seems to be a natural field,
> but I know it is hermetic space,
>
> a crystal formed in air, inside.
> I go among the silent trees
> and breathe their golden height.
>
> Having entered the unseen, I left
> my books and papers on the path
> to testify that someone took the step.
>
> "The Step"

There was, of course, nothing unusual about a young poet imitating Roethke in the 1960s. What made Ms. Quenneville remarkable was the quality of her imitations; some of them are indistinguishable from their models. And some of them are improvements:

> I weave a net
> line by line
> and tie a knot,
> and tie a knot;

5

cord by cord
I cross each space
and slip the string,
and slip the string.

When it is done,
line and cord,
I throw it over,
I throw it over
both our shoulders.
You see through
and the poem lets go;
the poem lets go,

the net starts over.

"The Weave"

Ms. Quenneville addressed or dedicated a number of poems to Roethke over the years. And yet her apprenticeship to him was very brief, to the point of nonexistence. Some of her best original work was actually written before these imitations; she was never overpowered by his influence. With him, she obviously shared a sense of the formal demands of poetry, as well as a fascination with the imagery of nature, but she had merely to loosen his strict forms and perfect rhymes to make her poems:

In the pine forest
the low thatches hang,
each needle like tallow,
green as a June bug's wing.

from "Pine Forest"

Many of these early poems were quickly accepted by some of the finest magazines in America. Ms. Quenneville found herself, a few years after Bentley's class, an established poet with a manuscript ready for publication, enrolled in a class taught by Elizabeth Bishop:

> I was one of the "awfully nice" students
> in your first writing class in Seattle
> whose "trouble all along
> was iambic pentameter."
> You called me to your office
> and tapped a meter on the table
> with your crooked fingers:
> "—ty, umpty, umpty, ump, get it?"
> I did and didn't.

from "Loving Relations"

The class went well. Ms. Quenneville began circulating her manuscript among the university presses, and she formed a friendship with Ms. Bishop sufficient enough to maintain a correspondence over several years. But then, a year from graduating, came the great turning point in her life: she was forced to quit school. The manuscript of poems was rejected everywhere, except at Louisiana State University Press, which desired the written opinion of a well-known poet on her work. Ms. Quenneville immediately wrote to Ms. Bishop, who responded:

> You will be surprised or disappointed or relieved—or a
> bit of all three, perhaps—to learn that I just received
> your letter of July 11th two days ago, here. It went to
> San Francisco and was eventually forwarded from there
> to Brazil by someone, I'm not sure who, by boat mail, I
> think. Then it was forwarded to me, airmail, to here, by
> the young man who is staying in my house in Ouro
> Preto. This all seems to have taken almost 3 months. I
> am awfully sorry because I certainly would have written
> a "plug" for you, as you call it.

Rarely has the tardy mail caused such damage. LSU Press, receiving no recommendation, rejected the manuscript and Ms. Quenneville took the silence of her former teacher for a judgment of her work. Bereft of her diploma and her book, she experienced "one of the strongest defeats" of her life. The dream of publishing a book was abandoned, as were literary friends who were no doubt bewildered at her gradual silence. (That she found the aesthetic distance to transform this story, some twenty years later, into the amusing poem "An Airletter from Elizabeth Bishop" is one of the minor triumphs of her art.) Nevertheless, Ms. Quenneville continued to write and to send poems to unknown editors at random magazines sporadically, which brings us to the packet that arrived in my mailbox that fall day.

These are the delineations of the poetic career, of course, not the poetry. Over the years a more private development was allotted to her than to her more famous classmates and that isolation forced her inward, forced her poetry into the personal, and finally into the spiritual. She had an enthusiasm for Eastern religions, traveling as far afield as India, looking for the answers she needed, and some of her best work is set there, written in various ashrams and temples.

Unsurprisingly, however, *childhood* became the great source of Freda Quenneville's work, her own childhood spent in rural Georgia. Nature poets, particularly, in fusing private concerns to universal images and personal feelings to inanimate matter often find individuality in the most common places: that is, after all, the primary mode of their expression. For such questions about the nature of things, such a search for identity, inevitably becomes the search for origins. So the path of her adulthood, from monasteries in Dharamsala to her beloved Ocmulgee River, was not circuitous but almost linear so far as the life of the imagination is concerned. Thus, the young poet would write —

> Birds, leaf by leaf, unfold
> from the live-oak tree;
> squirrels rise like smoke.
> The acorn's dark gold
> stays warm against my cheek.
> It is difficult to hold
> the vision of a child;
> my river is the world.
>
> "Scroll"

and then return, thirty years later, to expand on the same theme in her maturity —

> A child who knows a river, who by luck comes back
> from its depths — hands clutching moss as precious
> to her as the lily of immortality to Gilgamesh —
> is transformed by what flows and flowers through her;
> is freed into the mysteries, an Orpheus
> whose severed head, singing, floats downstream —
> a river's end too far to see —
> adrift on what was and will be.

from "The Child Who Saved Nature"

not simply because the elaboration of certain images was her central preoccupation as an artist, for that tells us nothing, but because the artist took these images for the very emblems of her life as a woman. And that is why her verses so often, as her friend Duane Niatum has written, "reveal the way childhood nourishes and guides us back to the origins of our ancestors, which is another way of saying the world of the universal soul."

But I am writing reminiscence, not criticism. And, in truth, I have provided the reader with only the crudest facts of Freda Quenneville's life because I did not know her well myself. Less than a year after we first exchanged compliments, she mentioned receiving some physical therapy for a case of tendonitis. Two months later, she had been diagnosed with a cancerous tumor, a slipping vertebra in her back, and "some garden variety disc degeneration." I do not remember being overly alarmed, principally because *she* was so calm, so sure that her illness was really a blessing, and "merely the prelude to a new phase of my career as a poet and whole person." I remember writing back, and waiting. Two months after this, a very different letter arrived.

What caught my attention first was that it was handwritten. The hand was not rushed, and the blue line was steady as it wrote, "in February I learned that the cancer had spread to my bone marrow, in the pelvis" and "fortunately, my oncologist is not one to give timelines." I was shocked. Perhaps I was even more shocked by her demeanor, as she quickly glossed over her prognosis to discuss the poems she was writing:

> These things are, of course, so interesting and exciting to me that I am much too busy to worry about my illness or how grim the reaper is. As long as I create my poems (and now I'm doing water color paintings too) I am living my life as I want to live it—and therein lies the great potential for health and healing. And I have promised myself that even if I get a complete and total cure tomorrow, I will not return to my job, which I so disliked and which cramped my soul. Part of me believes it is the unexpressed, unlived poet/artist in me who had to get the cancer so I could find a way to live my true life.

She was ebullient to the end, and it was not feigned. She wrote and painted in her death-bed. Surely, she did so in the faith that Art could heal Life, which is a common enough belief among artists. Mainly, though, I think she did so because she knew that art constituted her true life, that her life was *in* the writing. In this regard, I consider her an example for us all, and am honored to have been her friend and editor, all too briefly. Freda Quenneville died on the tenth of July, 1996. She was fifty-nine.

— *Garrick Davis*

PART I

Georgia Childhood

Don't think destiny's
more than what's packed
into childhood.

RAINER MARIA RILKE

One Heart, Last Seen

in Georgia. It had
the shape of a sassafras root
clutched warm in a grubby hand;
a bucketful of catawba worms
wreathed in a slithering mass
is how it felt;
it could hold about as much
as crayfish seines;
the sound of it was
June bugs on thin strings,
and it was fragile, too, pellucid
as the web of the writing spider
that scratched doomed names
from the holly to the front lawn swings.

Song

I want to go gathering
threads and cotton scraps in a gunny sack
and make a boll the weevils can't tell;
gather pine seeds
      that start flight but end,
      wings pinned in spider webs
      or wedged in bark, and remain
      to shudder a thin singing
      when the creek breathes
      and dirt cools under hot leaves.

I want to go gathering
tobacco bound in sheaves with stout twine
and hung on racks in sheds with fires in July;
gather dirt roads
      and the heat the sun baked
      into them, the bareness the wind
      blew onto them, the dust that coughed
      from them when I walked,
      tough-soled, alone,
      to the ends of them.

I want to go gathering
locust shells crusted on trunks, back seams split
with coming death, grim vacancies of skin and years:
I will gather them
      and thorns and beggar lice,
      wasp nests, bramble vines,
      maypops and rabbit dung;
      I will collect the negligible and mean
      until the wooden air is pierced
      with thin song.

Fire at Fair Oaks

Through twilight huddled in cool bunches
Beneath the oaks, my father walked up the dusty
Road, pulling the wagon I sat in. I wanted
To see the fire, and yet not. At three, I'd had
None of the dreams, which, proving nightmares real,
Prepare us to see ordinary terrors as pale shades
Of the eternal disturbances. We turned right
At the corner; the color of flames smote my eyes,
And streams of smoke rivered with the wind.
The cross-currents casting adrift black flakes
Like looming spiders on a webless sky.

My face burned hot as men hurled buckets of well
Water that sizzled against the flames like spit.
People dared in and out to salvage what they could;
Someone yelled, They got a mattress. Everyone
Cheered, as if it were sport to see how much
Can be saved, even when you're losing. I hid
My face away from flames in the nearest arms.
There's nothing we can do, my father said.
A man ran up and took my wagon careening
Behind him across the grass-lumped lawn.
When it came out of the home, its red paint glowed
As it bore to safety crockery and linen.

While fire licked limply at the grass, I headed
Through darkness heavy on the cooling dust,
Tugging the rusted wagon's hulk behind me;
And my thoughts fought with every turn of swollen
Wheels, for I, as faithless as the dust puffed
Upon my footsteps, was so near to learning
What was lost, and going home.

Hurricane at Bayou Teche

A stout-boxed house hewn from cypress
logged from the primeval swamp,
with an encircling porch and shuttered
long windows, the house Grandfather built
has been demolished by the envelope
I unglue from a relative's executrix kiss.

I never knew him, only what he's left,
old home turned insurance paper.
His wife, named Angel, had beaded veins
in her arms and legs and fed the chickens
just before she returned to heaven.
Long ago, her mother, over a hundred,
wore her bloomers across her spotted wrist
the whole hot day and, blinking like a vulture,
lifted bright objects which she dropped
from her claws forever into an attic trunk.
One Christmas, she made off with my gift,
a silver charm bracelet. Not even tears
could beg her, who spoke only French.

Across the pasture, dark-breathed shacks
for men who whacked the cane crops down
in rippling brown skin stood vacant,
except when we tried ghost stories before
a jury of mosquitoes. And the cistern,
a huge-staved barrel, dominated the yards
gaining rain, the only decent water.
When I was six, and we were visiting,
my first tooth came out. To rinse it,
I pulled the plug from the spigot
instead of turning it; and against

the spouted flow my hands were useless.
Half the cistern-trove wasted;
my tooth was lost in mud.
I got a spanking; that hundred-year-old
great-grandmother pronounced me Evil,
and my mother didn't explain how easily
a century does things to a person.

I smooth out the envelope with its paltry
claim and gather my eyes into all I cannot see.
Over that flat land a wind has swept
unrestrained, has leveled the grand cypress
hand-hewn vessel, uprooted storm cellars,
crushed shutters. The rotting cabins cast
their roofs skyward as the hurricane
rode out of the sea in a straight sheet;
and surely the cistern flooded before it burst
its hoard upon the mud my fingers seined
for a tooth. From an old trunk, my age-
encrusted bracelet was flung to rest
in infested swamps. Far away, inside,
I hear the wind beat doors, doors, doors,
before they vanish from their hinges.

A Pig Tale

Some elements shock and freeze us as we are.
Lucky for the suckling runt,
There were warm hands to take his part.
From my Aunt's bountiful sow
I had claimed him for a pet,
Bedded him in straw on the garage floor,
Proffered milk in Coke bottles topped with foolers.

He fed fat on the puffed edge of summer;
Gnashed, each day, a new nipple to shreds
In his sideways shank of raw teeth
And, pink and grunting
As he nosed my path,
Disgraced the cat-kept neighbors.

The cold snap that leveled November's dawn
Did him in.
I picked the body up from straw,
Kicked past doors
And bore him platter-like into the kitchen.
Stiff as a plank, we all agreed,
A candidate for pig heaven.

Mama, with last-ditch dispatch,
Threw open the oven
And shoved him on the rack.
Outside the closed door we waited,
Then heard at last a thin squeak,
A rattle, a sizzling squeal;
And the stilled blood took beats.
What the frost had left a pig,
Three minutes in the oven had delivered up,
Astonished, disgruntled, — saved.

The Boars

Nudging ahead of each other,
tearing our knees on thorns
and sliding downhill rump-on-mud,
fears as loud as our heads,
we shoved beyond ourselves toward
the creek hollow where wild boars lived.

Deep-nostrilled, snorting in narrow heads,
they rushed through trees of bramble,
eyes like the points of two rocks
struck in summer, spine bristles stiff
in the clattering leaves,
a grotto of noise left behind them
at the foot of the hill.

Crouched in the higher foliage,
we aimed sticks at their hides of thong.
They barreled at the air, in the clearing,
tusks lifted from thrown heads,
aping the rumbles of low August thunder.

The flint-wild eyes and sharp hooves
retreated into the sunless humid lair,
the labyrinth of blackberry bushes
and scuppernong vines where they hid.
We watched them, until the last one:

We knew how to rout them out
in the oppressive heat of the sun;
we had seen their shape, their eyes,
the texture of their skin.
We knew the madness lay within.

Ocmulgee Winters

The needles of the pines sloped down
Bearing burdens of great drops
At the end of each spine
Like mirrored globes of world
Turning on a point of green;
We used to touch them to our tongues
And drink a cool dew, turpentined;
When we shook the cones, water scattered
From secret sheds in rain-dark hulls,
Enough to wet one's clothes,
To say he'd been in a rainfall.

Wide puddles lulled in roadway ruts
And rain sluiced through every gully,
Piling old leaves and dried weeds
From the six-months parching summer
Into beavery mounds by hillside ditches;
The eaves of the house grew heavy
With old bird nests filled with water;
Troughs in barnyards freshly brimmed,
And shaled clay soaked itself soggy.

We wrapped schoolbooks in oilcloth
Too worn to be used on the table;
Wore boots for trudging to the bus stop
And, while we waited, gathered branches
For a fire that barely warmed us
But smelled of hickory and summer.

On weekend mornings I woke
To the sounds of rain and thunder:
Under the roof, I looked through windows —

Water sliding down panes in columns
On its way to the swell of the river,
Ocmulgee, "muddy water,"
Stream sweeping her winter cargo
Of rotten roots and timber,
Dead snakes, beer bottles and paper,
And I heard my parents talk of flooding
Down where the banks were lower.

It rained as it had rained for days;
Everything drained to the river.
Back in my bed of hand-quilt covers,
I listened and waited for sleep,
Deep in my nest beneath the dripping eaves,
Inward on my island
Beside the flooding waters.

Looking Through Minnows

Squatting between a sassafras and a willow,
I watched minnows fin under skinless water
Where the rocks pooled apart from the river
And held the fish flicking back and forth
Beneath the sun shattering upon my face.

I stayed watching, but not thinking of them,
Trying to feel what the usually jovial doctor,
Who always greeted me as the gal with the finest
Shoulders in the county, had said the day
They brought him home: He almost died. Now
Your father's got to have absolute quiet.
You see to it you don't upset him, h'm?

It all went back to that cold morning when
He got up to make the fire and suddenly fell,
His face as grey as ashes on the opened grate.
They called it thrombosis. I thought he just
Couldn't take it, getting up once more
To build a fire he'd been lighting fifty years.

The water in the pool I watched was dew-drop clear,
Not like the mudded channel it had flooded from.
And when the sun started slanting at the water,
It somehow got under it and shined upon the fish
In such a way they were transparent—a dark-cored
Middle with their inner workings visible.

I scooped a Louisianne can through the stream
And collected several of the flashing fish.
Then I hurried up the bank towards home,
Because it was wonderful to be able to see

Through something, to understand it.
And I'd bring them to him: I thought
It would be quiet, looking through minnows.

I whispered to Mama who guarded the door
With close-bunched eyes and rapid hands.
She said I'd better not disturb so much.
I hissed that you could see through fish.
My father heard and said, Let her come in.

I walked with careful feet placed one
By one to keep the swirling water still,
Tightening my fingers upon the rim so hard
They slipped and pinched on thin dry air.
The can clattered across the floor, and water
Pooled on polished tile as filmy fish flipped
And gasped; and the smile that I had felt,
My pride, was weighted lead, for in that room
The minnows died, and I knew I or the sun
Had lied, because I could not see through them.

The Split in the River

The sun was not always
    Warming my side;
Sometimes the river bent
    Under the shade,
And morning vined the banks
    Still dewed
With the grip of night.

Dark pines across from me
    Patched the clay
And fell aside where power
    Poles were staked.
A high island, stretched
    On the river's way,
It was a refuge for game.

In a flat-boat I'd helped
    Nail and tar,
My half-brother poled across
    The eroding river,
Dodging shoals, to spend his
    Weekends where
He was always in the shadow.

From the side I wandered,
    Gathering muscadines,
I shouted Brother! Brother!
    Out of sight,
He never answered. Tangled in
    His own vines,
He only shored a boat.

Older by years than I,
    He could drift
Alone; it was our mother
    He left.
Often in the night, I watched
    The island forest,
Saw his camped fire burn late

Against what fear or animal
    Tracked him there
Like Christ across the water;
    And in that dark,
I knew he drank boiled coffee
    That no sugar
Quenched, it was so bitter.

The Shot Across Water

Sundays, hot and still.
Not even the wisteria
catching a breeze,
the pine needles dry
and the maypops withered.
The tobacco weed bleached,
crackling in the fields.
The hills thundering
the silence of the sun,

and my brother walked out,
down the bank to the river,
loaded his rifle and stood.

Shoulders flexed, he cast
a tall shadow in the quiet
where minutes ticked over,
releasing the cartridge;
then sighting the ripple
that wavered against
the sweep of the current,
he squeezed the trigger.

The deep hills and pines
repeated the blast;
the ricochet on stones
chained the shot across water.

The snake and its motion
churned with the river,
its silence broken.

A Catch of Crawfish

My brother fished the river,
hunted with guns and traps;
but I and Sammy and Robert,
filling the deep summer days,
made seines from croker sacks
split open and nailed
to a pair of stilt-size sticks.

We seined the nameless creeks;
the springs that drained the hills,
the walnut groves and muscadines
as long ago as the Cherokees
and as near as our fingertips.

In unmoved pools where leaves
cast clear shadows under trees,
we poked and probed with the seine;
it was a gift of sense
how we could gauge,
at the dark bottom under boulders,
the proper tilt and twist of the sticks
that flipped the plundered crawfish
back in the trailing net;
and how, bringing it from the depths,
we would skim the tiny bream
from the shadows at the top; our cream.

We swung the lifted seine up high;
the water sieved as fast
as molten light through glass,
until, bereft of their element,
the crawfish bubbled silver in the air

among jumping wide minnows,
head-sluggish tadpoles
and streaks of eels:
our bright cauldron boiled—
sunlight, steam rising as it poured;
the seined catch singing.

The Fireflies

After a day's hot play
in the sun's long song
and nearly thirsting half to death,
their chests swelling
in and out of sharp ribs,
their heavy sweat hideously sweet,
the children dropped their steps to rest.

The bigger ones giggled in the glider
and sped the rusty chains,
while the old folk in rockers
padded their cooling bare feet;
and either the boards on the porch
or the rockers squeaked
like counting mice, and the talk
was squawked laughter, with mild pauses
before questions; but the young ones
squatted on the steps at the foot of the earth,

jostling, leering, listening when conversation
perked their dusty ears.
Shadows rose up from the trees to cool their toes;
like alert animals, their noses
waded into the light as it fell dim,
hung caught and smooth in yellow,
then settled blue across the weeds and fields
and drenched the backs of farther pines.

The glider slowed its pitch, laughter
dropped its jaw, and all across the porch
the boards or rockers faintly hummed.
The blue grew deep as oasis in heavy weeds;

cow bells rang slow full steps home;
and the children set their eyes
wide against the falling sky.

Up from the weeds and fields
the fireflies budded in wet, fresh Marches;
deep in the horizon, one by one,
they struck their small mating flashes
until the weeds caught fire
and the fields of silence blazed;
and the children, shivering awake
in that late, most final hour,
sat taken behind the rivers
of their eyes.

Rainy Season

There is a hush
        that gathers around
the leaky window frames;
        stately air: birds
all under a leaf or a wing,
        snails under stones;
squirrels and foxes asleep;
        mosquitoes and bees
flown back to sources of sound;
        the trees soaked brown.

Only woodsmoke stirred
        from a nearby fire
moves and rises and waits.
        Not clouds, — as clouds
in summer puff along horizons
        in a rolling train —
but one spreading drift of mist
        brings in the rain.

All day, all night, all week,
        evenly sieved,
the sky descends, enormously
        patient; not a crevice
and leaf are missed, but seep
        with quietness.

Rain all night drips over
        the roofs and windows,
making the sounds of the season
        of lovers together

when fields have been planted,
the forests are silent,
and the rain keeps falling
like a native chant.

Magnolia

I grew by
   Magnolia, lovely
as skin; in summer
it was heavened
in stars, green sky;
winter never
dimmed its shining.
When we moved,
stronger veins
were silent in the clay.

Haven't I
lived by others,
twined arms, limbs
in rooted shelters,
known the whelms
of deeper skin?
Why grow
   Magnolia, lovely,
draining flavor
from all that blossoms?

Root Garden

One Spring, I lowered myself into a cellar
of plants wintering under isinglass, —
a grave-sized niche in the earth
where Mama's begonias, tomatoes and azaleas

waited with guano in beds of straw, rain-
drenched and maturing in heated odors;
and there, beneath the sagging sun-crazed
roof, surrounded by clay pots bearing tubers

and shoots soon to be resurrected
beside the door and garden posts, I lay
in the fortuneless palm of death
watching a fly's slow climb from lethargy.

The wind siphoned away the air above me;
I breathed like a root with the clay and the cuttings.

The Weave

I weave a net
      line by line
and tie a knot,
and tie a knot;
      cord by cord
I cross each space
and slip the string,
and slip the string.

When it is done,
      line and cord,
I throw it over,
I throw it over
      both our shoulders.
You see through
and the poem lets go;
the poem lets go,

the net starts over.

Little Robert

You were my uncle, Little Robert,
but I never knew you existed
until yesterday when a visiting cousin
told me your story. You were
my father's youngest brother,
part of the pain he kept in silence.
You were seven, coming back from town

with your father on the tractor he'd bought
to work his cane crops in the bayous.
He (my grandfather, known
only in old photographs as a man
as dashing as Maurice Chevalier
in his dark suit, hat brim at an angle)
pulled up the tractor in front

of the big house, set the hand brake
and left the motor running
while he ran inside for a moment
(perhaps to tell Grandmother Hebert
he was back and was heading out
to the fields, maybe to grab his hat
or change his shirt, I don't know what),

but it was only a few minutes
that he asked you to wait for him, Little Robert.
And you, seven, an age more inventive
than patient, pretended to be
the driver and pulled on the brake lever.
The tractor jolted and threw you to the ground,
then lurched over you, blades turning,

and cut your body into little pieces.
O Little Robert! Think
of Grandfather coming from the house
and down the steps to find you
spent like milled stalks of sugar cane
in the front yard. Think of Grandmother,
tugging at the wispy strands of hair

escaping from the bun at the back
of her neck, making the sign of the cross
and falling to her knees
in the holocaust of your body,
like a hen gone mad with the task
of gathering a hundred chicks to her nest.
Little Robert, I didn't know you

until yesterday, and then you died
as suddenly as if I myself had just walked
out of the house and found you threshed
alive in the front yard. Is that
the very place where Grandmother
planted a rose garden, enclosed
in a fence like a shrine?

It was so peaceful there,
full of blossoms even in December.

June Bugs

Georgia. Outdoors all day,
June bugs in summer,
and Sammyandrobert on the porch
whining, "What can I do?"
This morning, I think of them.
June bugs. How to explain?
The shiny, bronze-green
flash hunted in the grass,
tied by a leg with a thread.
Pull the knot too hard—
the leg fell off.
Never mind, it had others.

Secured, the June bugs droned
above our heads,
taking the air like stairs
that weren't there
and never would be.
They flew better than airplanes,
better than Christmas wind-up toys.
We never stopped to think
what use we put them to;
never counted the missing legs.

Seattle. Rain again,
and God, I'm like a June bug
at the end of my thread.
No telling how many limbs
I've had to sacrifice
to other creatures' clumsiness.
But those June bugs,
they made me happy

in the dense, relentless
childhood summer;
they sang an ancient,
chained and longing sound
that shivered in my veins.
I can hear it still,
and still, it sings.

PART II

Dark Comfort

I spread pages over me like layers
of healing scar to strengthen walls.

Who can outlive their childhood?
My needs create me; I am growing
into something I do not understand.
Sometimes, it is beautiful.

FROM "Visions of Mercy, Songs of Locusts"

Having Begonias

Mama spent hours tending her begonias,
she kept a porch full of them.
I couldn't see what she got out of it.
They were plush and lovely;
she was ill, maybe manic-depressive
or schizophrenic, alternately
hung out in juke-joints,
drank like a fish, danced,
swore and whored like a sailor
when the whim hit and, sober,
tried to kill herself.
But her begonias thrived.
Figure it out.

She's long dead, my four kids
are grown and gone (one of them
permanent at the State Hospital),
and my exhusband took my inheritance
because he said he was the one
went to work every day and bought
the groceries. My daughters
think I'm overpowering,
but I'm only being myself,
which is basically sedentary.
What's so strong about that?

I go to work every day,
come home alone and read.
I worry about schizophrenia
showing up in the grandchildren.
I don't know why, but lately
I've been thinking about begonias

so last week I bought
a whole gang of them for the lanai.
Their cabbage-dimpled faces—
blush, salmon, apricot and rose—
look like they're smiling.
I admit it makes me feel
at home and normal,
having begonias.

Conch Shell

There was a conch shell
as far back
as my memory goes.
My father held it to my ear
and said, "Listen,
you can hear the ocean."

I was three or four;
I'd never seen an ocean,
but I could hear sounds
that would be wind and waves,
when I'd learned them.
My father had found

the conch in the sea,
the creature dead inside.
He buried it for years
to cure its odor.
It became a door stop
at the end of the hall,

where dust gulls
soared in the sunlight.
By the time I was twelve,
I'd seen two oceans;
they sounded like conch shells
breathing in my ear.

The June I was sixteen
my father died.
The wind darkened;
I could hear sea terns

keening inside the shell
at the end of the hallway.

I moved away alone;
the conch shell sank
in memory, like a creature
thrown back to the sea,
lost to the slow
silt of years.

It returns, decades later,
when the wind blows
through open doors in summer,
the shell of invisible
oceans pressing my ear,
my father saying, "Listen. . . ."

Yellow Tulips

for Teresa

The potted yellow tulips
stand at attention,
bright and unyielding,
as if they had to be
that stubborn
to break the ground.
Don't all survivors
have the same
no–nonsense air?

Early spring in Seattle,
choirs of rain
sing to waken
the death-mask sun
in time for Easter.
But it rarely happens
in these northern latitudes. . . .

One Easter we visited
the Woodland Zoo.
You wore your new coat
(red, with gold buttons)
and a white fur muff.
You tried so hard
to be adult.

It was April, cold as
now. I bent down
to button your coat—
a small but graceful act.

Looking back,
I'd swear I loved you.

. . . In time for Easter
in these northern latitudes,
blossoms must be forced
in greenhouse heat.
The real air chills,
like leaning long
against bare granite;
like seeing your final self.

O seed, forgive the earth
through which you passed,
are passing still,
impelled by a sun
that is half unseen, unknown—
or hidden wholly
in yellow tulips.

Lullaby to a Grown Daughter

The crackle of crickets,
the lapping leaves,
a butterfly's silence,
the droning bees.

The creek is sighing
on its way to the sea;
you have lost your lover,
you are lost in dreams.

I watch the aurora
borealis stream.
I am your mother,
who taught you to dream.

Rain

The rain
comes down
with the rain

sometimes it thunders
like the fierce Chimera

and rattles
the roof
like hoof-beats on stone

sometimes it mists
like the breath
of Pegasus climbing—

a colophon
painted so thin
you can barely hear

Bellerephon
sighing

Women Not Kept

Women not kept
work hard for what they get,

often not enough
money to live on, or love.

Long ago, as a wife,
she had enough to keep her alive,

like a body on machines
and tubes beneath hospital sheets:

vitals taken and given,
the good care of a safe haven.

She was resurrected,
made up and dressed to attend

each of her daughters'
graduations, weddings and childbirths.

From the last outing
she never returned. She wanted out;

she wanted freedom—
as if she would never learn the lesson

women not kept
have learned, and learning, wept.

The Choice

The choice, once made, is as keen
as a blade of ice,
as clear and unforgiving.
Though worlds of dream and grace
exist, and other ways of being,
I am forced to choose
my common drudgery, my terror,
the memories I encode
in boredom or in error,
the best route to the grocery store,
the highest rate of interest;
in short, my survival and my fitness.
Then I must also choose
what the choice denies —
the visceral residue,
the part of me that dies.

Little Lessons

The rivulet, the stream, the river
are currents that cannot stop
what feeds them
or restrain the gravity
of their own impulsion. They
live by going where they go,
stone by stone moving mountains,
drop by drop gathering floods.

The rivulet, the stream, the river
absorb raw mud and earth
without thinking;
expose the roots of giant trees
whose seeds were formed
long before the shore was threatened
by rivers going
where they must go.

You are going. You will not know
the mountains are vacant,
the trees leaning
with nerve-roots loosened
as if they must fall.
Fall and follow
the element that was already gone
as soon as it was known.

Salmon La Sac River

We drive north of the Roslyn Cafe —
that "Oasis" now encroached upon
by Northern Exposure tourists —
and follow the twisting Salmon La Sac.

Oh, wilderness still exists
just two hours east of Seattle —
as remote as lost youth,
but remembered, like a geography lesson.

The Salmon La Sac, in its tumbled
canyon, is picture-perfect.
How many years was the river
alone in its wildness,

grinding rock and cedar, laddering
stones for returning salmon?
We stop beside the Salmon La Sac
and coax each other to wade in,

little by little, until
we are the same as the river,
threading the current like tadpoles,
peering into the stone-green silence.

Huge white-lily snow fields
bloom on the mountains,
the high meadows teem
with wildflowers and thistle,

the forests ripple with
bird calls and horse flies.
But all the wild salmon
are gone.

Seattle Spring

The star magnolia's bloomed and gone.
The chestnuts have unwrapped
their green candles,
the lindens their hearts of green.
Plum blossoms hang from boughs
like excess lace;
fading tulips tip their cups
like woozy wedding guests,
and wait.
This is only April;
it will go on and on, —
more greening, more blooming
and pigeons preening;
it will be one build-up after another,
with no arrival at fullness
and declamation
in sight.
Through July,
it will be Spring,
alert and verdant, not quite cold,
but far from warm—like a bridesmaid deferring
to the bride.
The sun won't hit
its stride till August;
in two weeks the brush will turn to sage
and the first yellow leaf will startle,
it falls so soon.
But Summer's only started!
you exclaim, and what
were all those green months for,
if not to usher in a haze
of warm, climactic lushness?

Ah, the Seattle Spring is slow
and green, beautiful as no other,
but cool as a soul
that does not give way to passion gladly, —
or almost too late.

Dark-Eyed Fuchsias

The closed buds hang like bright buoys
in vertical harbors, Chinese
lanterns in miniature trees.

Mature, the stamens pierce
through lantern-tips, their slim candles
extruding the dust of consumed suns;

then the dense, inner-wimpled petals
split the lightless globes
into wings, the upcurled tiers
of painted pagodas—

and blossoms at first as crumpled
as the face of a newborn child
unfurl their origamis, puzzle-
perfect every time.

Afternoon Art at the Rainier Club

for Mary Randlett

I take time off from my job (an hour
and a half's vacation) to see the paintings
at the Rainier Club—a British Raj-like
(though more gently-faded) enclave
of carved, hammered, polished taste,
three blocks north of the County Building
I've just come from. Mary has invited me here
with four other friends to see the paintings
and her photographs of the men who made them.
Their path is through the needle's eye of art.

The early afternoon Spring light streams
through arched windows and leaded panes
into a balanced inner atmosphere.
The boom of traffic and construction noises
on Fourth Avenue can't enter over
the ubiquitous symphonic music laid
on the air as deftly as the Persian carpets
in the great colonnaded day room,
which has a fireplace big enough to camp in.

I have just left the office where I work
for Roads and Engineering, an office
full of paper dust and dead cells
falling from the bodies of a hundred
engineers crammed into padded cubicles
(task modules, they call them);
an office the size of a city block,
rarely vacuumed and never polished,
the air a depleted 80 degrees

even on this blue-breeze afternoon—
where I must soon return.

My gaze plays over the paintings
like the Spring light that will not stay,
but touches and holds them fleetingly
before it turns gray again
with tomorrow's rain: Callahan's epiphanies,
Anderson's figures evoking cathedrals,
Tsutakawa's calligraphies of space,
Tobey's cellular galaxies dividing inward forever
and Graves' "Bird with Possession"—
    O rara avis, what did *you* possess,
brooding alone with your egg of art,
the grain of gold clutched in hungry talons?

I take what I can remember, like keys
and coins and visa stuffed into a purse,
before I return to the Spring air
that will give way to rain tomorrow,
to the torn pavement and traffic noise
on Fourth Avenue, to the County office and, later,
to my unpolished life, to the poem
I must trade my sleep to write,
and to something, in spite of all that,
as ineffable as rain followed by light.

An Airletter from Elizabeth Bishop

It was three months travelling from Ouro Prêto,
Brazil to Seattle, and that was puzzling enough,
but how it looked! crumpled and torn,
as though it had made its way through deep
jungle stuck to the sole of the postman's sandal.

I imagine it thus: he noticed the airletter
flapping (this down-at-the-heel winged Mercury)
and thought to smooth it out across his belly,
snagging three holes down its center
on the metal tooth of his belt buckle, neat
as a hooked fish.

                    He took it home
to flatten overnight between the stones
his wife used for grinding corn—where two
of its corners were rasped and beaten
into the evening tortillas.

                    Next day, as
the postman saw the airletter flying
across the yard with sparring roosters,
he wondered, Now what, mail it or not?
and placed it in the family Bible
for safekeeping (awaiting guidance).

Two months later, when his third child was born
and the event recorded in the holy pages,
the airletter fluttered out. (Like the wan-
dering Jew, survival lay in moving on).
The typed address was still good.

The postman took it to the *correio*
and, crossing himself, stuck it inside
a mail sack bound by rail for Rio.
A week later, the airletter was bundled
onto a Boeing jet—a horse of home
that knew its way back.

It travelled
rather quickly, then, to the mailbox
at my door. It looked as used as sin.
Carefully I slit the remaining edges
of flimsy, pale air paper.

Opened, it
appeared to be a jungle primitive's
idea of a kindergartner's snowflake.
Of the tightly typed, margin-to-margin words,
one in six was missing or corrupt—
probably those she'd pondered longest.

PART III

The Journey East

In India, the fruit vendors arrive
before dawn, spread bright cotton blankets
along dusty village roadways,
and carefully arrange their custard apples,
papayas, sweet limes, masambis,
and jack fruit in stacks
like little towered temples.

FROM "A Kilo of Mangoes"

On the Way to Dharamsala

Two-thirds through an 18-hour trip
by dusty, rickety bus—
past Chandigarh and Mandi,
before we ascend
to the Kangra Valley—
we make another curl
in the tattered roadway
and come upon a sudden
opening in the hills.

             There
the Himalayas stand, a crowd
of jagged slabs of ice and snow,
like a wall upon the sky.

             High;
too high for me to climb—
but it is my home
and I am going there.
Not this day, this lifetime.
But in that distance.

Hostas

Like archives of summer,
hostas' broad leaves
are subtexts to the shade,
the gloss in flowered margins.
Toward the end of prime,
they launch tall styluses
to absorb the sun,
nubs tipped with buds
whose lily mouths open
as if to phrase the vowel in *love,*
then close around a tear.

Their slow green volumes
fade in autumn,
tropical fronds patined
and brittle
as the Shastri's
palm leaf manuscripts.

All living things are scrolls
of dust whose
mysteries we only guess:
how Vishnu ciphered the world
from a dream in his navel;
how Cleopatra shaped
Antony's oblivion
on a barge of blue dreams;
why I broke a branch
from the sentry tree
in a dream I can't recall.

Eucalyptus

Ootacamond
sits atop
the blue Nilgiris,
the aromatic spritz
of eucalyptus everywhere.
Ice in the morning water jugs,
rough shawls in the dawn.
A baby goat practices
mountain-crag stances
on a pile of uphill rubble.
The chi shop table top
is black — until the flies
take off, clearing a landing
for tea in heavy cups,
thick with sugar
and cardamom.

Today I boiled
eucalyptus leaves
in a kettle:
the baby goat runs
uphill with a clatter;
the flies settle
on the table top.
I drink the local tea,
breathe the spirited air.
I have not yet taken
the zigzag bus
downhill from the eucalyptus
into dense Trivandrum;
have not yet entered the jungle
that kneels in vain
by the sea.

Mango Delight

You remember home, where the sun rises
like a growing presence you open the windows for.
Here it boils up full strength:
one moment it's cool dim dawn,
then the sun strikes like a falling anvil.
(*Sunstroke* is not a misnomer.)

Dust swirls from the stripped earth
and hangs in the air like a tincture.
You breathe it day and night without thinking.
It won't settle till the monsoons
wash it from the sky and fling it
like wet laundry at your feet, faded and shapeless,
slippery as silk or handkerchief linen.

In the hot hours, natives return to homes
with walls of brick or wattle—fortresses
plastered inside and out with mud and mortar—
where the sun cannot follow, and sleep.
Foreigners rest fitfully in the noonday light:
they lounge in hotels over long teas,
read desultorily, and write letters
to loves remaining on other continents—
letters like indelible chapters in dream:

> Went to Anantapur to renew our visas.
> We were on a wide, main street
> full of bullock carts, taxis,
> auto-rickshaws, and cows with horns
> painted blood-red and yellow.
> We heard strange noises,—loud,
> guttural groans pierced by shrieks.

Virginia said, "What on earth. . . .
Look at that! Is it. . . ?"

It was a woman—or the head and trunk
of one—with no arms or legs,
swathed in dirt-stained rags,
lumping herself forward, worm-like,
along the edge of the macadam.
The rickshaws swerved in a shower
of horns, and the ponderous bullocks
lumbered past, just inches from her path
(if there *is* such a thing as a path
for a body without arms, legs, or feet).
Did she shriek from the assaults
of belly and chest on asphalt?
or did she scream to warn off cows
and bullocks and rickshaws?

God knows where she was going
or how long she'd been travelling.
"Never," said Virginia, "have I seen
a person brought so low. . . ."

$\sim$

The trip to Ooty was hot
and we made a long stop at Mysore.
I stayed on the bus (out
of the sun, but it was an oven),
watching people coming and going.
I noticed a tall thin boy
standing under a tree, his legs bare
and thin as two pencil lines,
with bulging parentheses for knees.
I couldn't help but stare.

He walked across the street,
as if on child's stilts,
and came to the window where I sat.
His eyes were patient and silent
and somehow compassionate.

Oddly, he didn't beg. Perhaps
he'd never seen a face as pink
and flushed with heat as mine.
Did he think someone so peeled
of pigment must be ill or dying?
I stared back, stunned
at his enduring presence,
and it never crossed my mind
to give *baksheesh,* for what,
in a world so outwardly thin,
could be of use to him—
looking like a great crane
whose existence does not depend
upon its paltry legs?
That's all I saw of Mysore.
I hope to stop there on the way back
and tour the Maharajah's palace,
the one with doors of solid silver....

The sun sinks deeper in the haze,
like a frayed ember too hot to touch
but dampered, now, without its crown of flame.
Shopkeepers raise corrugated metal doors, a kohl-
eyed woman hawks gaudy bangles near the chai stall,
and the jewelry merchant slips a magnifier
on his good eye and waits for wealthy Westerners.

From now until dinner, long after dark,
you spend the energy hoarded during hours of heat.
You walk through a village of thatched huts,

where dark children lean from dark doorways,
and you come upon a square—the heart of *somewhere*—
with its central tree (a *neem*) on a dais of earth
enclosed by rocks, and at its base,
simple stone gods and goddesses stand,
anointed with *ghee* and hung with flowers.
The elephant-keeper passes, leading Gita
to a pond in the bamboo forest.

You wander in the labyrinthine lanes
of an old bazaar; Kashmiri traders with snow-blue eyes
invite you in to sit on sumptuous carpets,
ply you with sheaf after sheaf of Garden tapestries,
and demonstrate ring shawls—those oblong yards
of wool so sheer they pass like prayer beads
through a ring from your finger.
You, or they, may or may not be back tomorrow.

You wind up in an almost-blind alley
where the ice-cream wallah's padlocked freezer
churns night and day, keeping cones and ices and something
on a wooden stick called "Mango Delight."
It costs eight Rupees (that year, a whole American dollar)—
a sorbet or sherbet of sun ripe mangoes,
peach-colored and sweet, so cold
and clean (as only tropical fruit is clean)
it clears your throat of dust at last.

Cold and clean, it slakes a craving
that hadn't yet announced its object
but, once discovered, there is no doubt
it's what you had desired since your first day in India:
the fruit of the triumphal,
terrible sun. Frozen, and wrapped
in clean-looking paper.

Dharamsala

This, too, is India—
a Tibetan village transposed
yak load by yak load
across time and glaciers;
refuge of the Dalai Lama.

Here, on the dirt road
winding past the lamasery,
prayer flags snap
like curtains in the wind,
sending *Om Mane Padme Hum*
around the globe,

and the chants of monks
unfold in layered tones,
the chords repeating
down mile-high mountains,
like the green declensions
of terraced slopes.

We walk along a road no wider
than a ledge in space;
cloud-thrown patterns
pace the valley below.
You have become an actor
in a dream I cannot place.

The Dhaula Dhar, in eternal snow,
stands halfway up the sky.
Blossoming cherries cast
a net across the depths;
pines and ban oaks lean
like madronas on the bluffs at home.

Was it only yesterday I learned
your face of love is false?
Prayer flags scribble *Om*
to the wind. Dry
scree rolls beneath my sandals
and ricochets down cliffs.

Our ascent is frozen here,
as if a bitter avalanche
had filled the road;
and I will climb many terraces
of green sleep, amid snows
as fast as the Dhaula Dhar,

until I reach the wind
where flags intone
Om Mane Padme Hum
and I step out of you, —
and the distant
chasm's closed.

Taj Mahal

Ironic,
this tomb for love
is now a state monument,

the once-
lavish crypts robbed
of gold and silver.

What remains
are jasper, lapis,
and carnelian flowers

inlaid
in a marble mausoleum.
What has endured

the Raj,
vandals, and acid rain
is the basic structure—

as if
to prove even
damaged or diluted,

love is
singular, perfect
as a poem.

Rituals on the Malabar Coast, India

There was an ocean between us,
daughter, and you followed.
Alone with time, I was trying to believe
there'd be an end to the tunnel
and daylight left for me.
We have lost each other's tempo:
fouled connections at the airport,
agendas that won't jibe.

At dawn on the Arabian Sea
we gather shells and sort them,
trained and cautious soldiers on the sand;
thick spikes of armor, crusted
warriors from the reef.
For days we barely speak.

The wind at the breakers' edge
keeps the mosquito hoards away.
I want to tell you that I am mortal
and you are wounding;
why waste your purpose stalking me?
A mother loves you into life
but cannot save you from it.

The last evening, we walk
as equidistant as the palms
that stagger down the headland,
tracking one another on the shore.
Ahead, a dozen brown men
stand knee-deep in water,
casting flower petals on the tide,

and serenely chant as the sun sets,
and wave their incense on the sky.

You stop and wait, as if you sense
what should not be disturbed,
but I wade in among the men,
who abjectly bow and move aside.
Visible now, the funeral ash,
thin as oil on water; a bit of dust
or flotsam in a drifting sea.

How small the final offering;
how gently the waves and blossoms move as one.

PART IV

Final Ascent

It was the dark of December
when I learned I was ill
and my life was a question.

FROM "Wings"

She doesn't require much
except a little food, frequent rest,
some old and some new photographs
and a few more years to watch
the memories shaping up
beyond the window,—the young self
she still studies like a text.

FROM "The Last Window"

The Log and the Light

One dead drift-log
lies black against the sand,
beached at the water line.
Rings of light spread out
from the log, as if the waves
are trying to wash it loose;
to send it drifting into the pool
of light that shimmers
below the dark horizon.

For all its lumpishness,
the log stands so lightly balanced
between sand and water—
like a dancer's leg on the bar—
you wonder it doesn't roll
into the next wave and float away;
for the log is being summoned
(you know it) by the dazzling adagios
of light playing across the water.

Here is the tension:
the dark, unused or useless stuff
of used-up matter is grounded,
while the light—that nonmaterial
energy on which our every thought
and deed depend—beckons
the hulk to rise, to dance, to swim,
to flow into being.

The log knows it must become
one with the source of that summons,
even if it takes a thousand years.

The light knows this too; knows
what time makes of fallen things.
The log and the light wait
for the ultimate shape
they will give to each other.

October Light

This will go on forever—
the burnished light of Autumn
sweeping the long grass
over the brow of a hill,
blackberries hanging dried on the vine,
clover blossoming among fallen leaves,
white clouds riding the blue wind,
Lombardy poplars making
golden brush strokes on the sky.

You never belonged to me;
I never belonged to you.
That, too, will someday change.
But this Autumn day will never end
because I have pictured it so,—
and I will go on forever,
in the cycling atoms of trees and light.
Then I will belong to you;
we will belong to each other.

The Sun at the Summer Solstice

The sun is always shining
on the cabin
beside the hummingbird woods
in the little town
of Randle;

always shining
on highway 25,
winding through forests
on the way to St Helens;

always shining on trails
through the blast zone,
the trees thrown like match sticks
down the sides of the hills—
some still surfing, jutting
over the next frozen wave.

The sun is always shining
on the broken crater,
and the dome is
sending endless smoke signals
to tribes far lost
and no longer shining—

like the sun
when the equinox comes.

Birthday Gift

I sat outside a cabin
in the woods at dark,
studying the stars

the way I did as a child
in the summer South—
feeling them, even loving.

As I watched, huge
swathes of light formed
triumphal swords

pointing to the apex
of the heavens, like ribs
of light vaulting

a domed cathedral,
and light poured,
as I imagined,

from the rose window
at Chartres lit
by the sun.

The shapes changed
to waves and billows;
it was the rare

aurora borealis—
something I'd never
hoped to see, further

from my Southern dreams
than the Taj Mahal,
the temple of Athena

or fantasy-
towered St. Basil's,
whose architect

the Czar had
blinded, never
to create its rival.

Harmony Trail

On the slope of a hill
on the shadow side of St Helens,
a vertical garden of moss,
fern and elderberry
grows in the blast zone.

Far below, broken
ghost trees stand
in rippled mud flows,
waiting for another century.

Harmony of green hills
and bare trees,
rhythm of lupine and fireweed
and gray-white pumice,
where a hummingbird hovers,
small as a thumbprint.

Startled, ashen logs
drift together,
a carpet
on Spirit Lake.

Steam rises from the crater,
immense with silence
and reflected glaciers.
Over the hillsides
white logs glisten,
silver flames
in the purple penstemon.

Blue Pearl

The silver clarity
of mountains is my roof,
moon-washed oceans are my floor,
the energy unleashed in fields of wheat
my bread and hearth,
the choiring wind my church,
wildflowers on the altar.

Perigee

The snow mountains are lit
with the morning sun,
visible through the winter trees
outside my door.

Last night the full moon
was twelve percent larger than normal,
thirty thousand miles closer to earth
at perigee.

       It stood at my window,
wreathed in haloes of frost breath,
a white stone in icy ripples.
One sun, one moon, tend our earth
and influence all its changes.

New snow on the far mountains,
the trees leafing and unleafing,
the moon sliding to apogee.
I am always changing
into what I am.

Washington Pass, North Cascades Highway

The firs on the granite precipice
spiral into themselves, roots embedded
in the latest outcroppings of geological time.
Far below, the highway bends its wing
beneath the crests of Kangaroo Ridge,
the Minutemen, and Liberty Bell Mountain.
The tiny, human veins of my being
are washed to nothing in auroral spaces.

My friend is content in this immensity
and says, "Who am I to worry?"
For hours our conversation has returned
again and again to perceptions of God.
What have words to do with
the gaping canyon in front of me,
the sheer drop hundreds of feet
from my center of gravity?
The absolute is known for its lack
of concrete nouns and images.

We drive from the pass and stop
at the Cascade River. In the sun,
a few yards downstream, a trout
breaks from the rapids in a one-shot body arc,
its mystery raised to eye
level an instant before it falls
back into the continuum of silt-dim water.
Twice I see it surface; he does not.
I know it must appear again—
the trinity law of occurrence.

I wade alone up a nearby stream,
a tree-lined cradle of minnows
in the sand of the flood plain.
God is not a question nor absence.
The simpler, personal need is for
a substance to constrain emotion—
clay or sponge to soak it up,
hold it like rain against drought,
the time of dry journeys.

When I return to the river's edge,
the trout leaps again—the third-
time charm, the little miracle,
the symbol of food for the senses,
the multitudes of them.

Diamond Light

Inspired by a photograph
by Mary Randlett

I stand at the head of an estuary
where sheer cliffs cascade
into the darkness far below,
the jagged edges outlined against the bay
like black paper cut-outs.

All the light is caught inside the water.
Near the beachhead lies another mass
of darkness — an island of rock
surrounded by the water's brilliant,
diamond-faceted shapes.

I stand on the cliff above the darkness,
above the light, on an edge no wider
than a pathway in the mind.
Here I can cling to the stability
of the cliff's dark surface, —
or I can let myself fall
through this thin paper cut-out scene
into the heaving light,
into the reality of the bay's cold water
and torturous, uncertain currents.

Shall I step off the cliff's edge
into the diamond light,
willing to become fully awake,
fully aware of the footing I have lost;
ready to follow the tide
wherever it flows?

The diamond light of the bay
leads to the ocean. Think.

Perhaps I am too incautious,
walking along these dark cliffs,
with the light sprawled in front of me
like an oasis of wellheads sprung
from the heart of the sun.
The light's pull is fierce,
too strong to resist.
Like the rarest of diamonds,
it exacts its price in wageless labor,
its fire born of the darkness
it consumes within.

Snoqualmie Falls

The crocuses are sprouting in Seattle
while in the mountains
the snow has grown transparent,
like the face of the very old,
lit beyond the wrinkled surface.

We watch the river pouring over the cliff
at Snoqualmie: jets and streams and aureoles
in patterns of surprising sameness,
newly transformed each second,
like fireworks that never expire.
This water stronger than fire.

Tourists crowd the lookout:
heavily-accented men with cameras
and silken, perfumed women —
honeymooners at Salish Lodge
above the Falls.

I feel myself floating across the chasm
into the disgorging river,
the waters rising in the air
to meet me where I stand.
For a moment I am no longer a person,
I am one of the dead,
one of the Snoqualmie
who knew the Falls as the Great Spirit,
and I grow sad, sad as though
I cannot live again, knowing the Falls
will one day vanish, and the last trace
of sacred earth go with it.

I am worried about many things:
how life is shrinking and I am dying to it,
like a drop in the great roaring river
on its run to the sea.
Perhaps my sorrow is that I
am no longer earth or fire.
I am water; old and impersonal,

like rivers
still clinging to earth,
still stronger than fire;
falling, but not yet born
to the fourth element.

Ocmulgee Jubilee

for Charles Hebert

I have celebrated the small
moons reflected in the river,
and veins of gray kaolin,
crackled quartz, arrowheads,
and tree trunks twigged with fur,
hidden along its edge.

The river has gone miles and years.
I have crossed dry lands and oceans.
And though the same sheen pours
over granite shoals where sun-
browned children played
and Charlie caught catfish,

no one looking down that lost
hillside can see the rough-
rouged and boulder-shagged
Ocmulgee River flowing.
It will die when I die—
its flinty moons of grace,

its isinglass minnows milling
in clear shallows, its far surface
glazed and breathing like a scar
amid a haze of midges,
where bass leap in a fling of pearls—
the whole unwritten jubilee.

FREDA QUENNEVILLE (1937–1996)
was an award-winning poet whose
works appeared in over forty magazines
including *The New Yorker, The Nation,
The Chicago Tribune, The Seattle Poetry
Review, Poetry Northwest,* and *Prairie
Schooner.* Born in Georgia, she attended
the University of Washington and lived
most of her life near Seattle. Her lyrics
were commissioned and performed
by the Sacred Earth Singers, the Seattle
Women's Ensemble, and the Vancouver
Women's Chorus. *Child of the Ocmulgee*
is her first collection of poetry.